Folens HISTORY
Primary Specials!
INVADERS, SETTLERS IN BRITAIN

941.01

Mary Green

Acknowledgements

Beowulf and the Monster by Brian Patten, Scholastic, 1999

Cover image courtesy of Mary Evans Picture Library

Bibliography

An Introduction to Anglo-Saxon England by Peter Hunter Blair, Cambridge University Press, reprinted 1995

© 2004 Folens Limited, on behalf of the author.

United Kingdom: Folens Publishers, Apex Business Centre, Boscombe Road, Dunstable, LU5 4RL

Email: folens@folens.com

Ireland: Folens Publishers, Greenhills Road, Tallaght, Dublin 24
Email: info@folens.ie

Poland: JUKA, ul. Renesansowa 38, Warsaw 01-905

Folens allows photocopying of pages marked 'copiable page' for educational use, providing that this use is within the confines of the purchasing institution. Copiable pages should not be declared in any return in respect of any photocopying licence.

Folens publications are protected by international copyright laws. All rights are reserved. The copyright of all materials in this publication, except where otherwise stated, remains the property of the publisher and author. No part of this publication may be reproduced, stored in a retrieval system, or transmitted, in any form or by any means, for whatever purpose, without the written permission of Folens Limited.

Mary Green hereby asserts her moral right to be identified as the author of this work in accordance with the Copyright, Designs and Patents Act 1988.

Editor: Dawn Booth
Illustrations: Tony Randell
Layout artist: Patricia Hollingsworth
Cover design: Martin Cross

First published 2004 by Folens Limited.

Every effort has been made to contact copyright holders of material used in this publication. If any copyright holder has been overlooked, we should be pleased to make any necessary arrangements.

British Library Cataloguing in Publication Data. A catalogue record for this publication is available from the British Library.

ISBN 1 84303 058 6

23819

Contents

Many Cultures — 5

The Celts and Romans
The Celtic Way of Life — 9

Celtic Art — 13

Boudicca — 17

The Roman Army — 21

The Roman Way of Life — 25

The Villa — 29

The Anglo-Saxons
The Sutton Hoo Burial — 33

The Sutton Hoo Treasure — 37

The East Anglian King — 41

Beowulf — 45

The Vikings
Who were the Vikings? — 49

The Viking Longship 1 — 53

The Viking Longship 2 — 57

Jorvik — 61

We hope you enjoy using this new *Primary Specials!* book, to be used with children achieving at a lower level. The book has been written in response to market research with teachers. The focus is a central resource that is entirely visual, with a few exceptions that are written resources, such as historical stories. Accompanying this are support materials. The book follows the revised National Curriculum for History (History 2000) and the QCA scheme of work at Key Stage 2.

New *Primary Specials!* contain 15 separate chapters, each covering a new topic within the theme of the book. The resource and activity pages are photocopiable and are accompanied by a page of notes for the teacher. This page is laid out as follows:

Background
– gives useful information on the topic, which the teacher can draw on as needed.

Working with the resource
– gives guidance on using the resource as the focus of group discussion, which should be led by the teacher or a support assistant. **Useful questions** are also included.

Using the activity sheets
– provides information on the differentiated tasks related to the resource. The activity pages often include graphic organisers such as spidergrams, writing frames and chronological and other models, to support pupils' thinking and recording.

Skills
Important historical skills are included across the books. These should be within the children's abilities, such as:
– promoting the sense of the passage of time
– sequencing events and promoting a sense of chronology
– distinguishing between simple fact and opinion
– recognising that while some things change others stay the same
– promoting empathy through identifying with lives in the past
– recognising simple cause and effect.

Why not look for these other titles in the series?

Ancient Egypt	FC0616
Ancient Greece	FC0640
Children in the Second World War	FC0608
Children in Victorian Britain	FC0624
Tudor Times	FC0594
How Life Has Changed Since 1948	FC0632

Can't find the topic you are looking for? If you have any ideas for other titles to be covered in the *Primary Specials!* series write and let us know:

Publishing Department
Folens Publishers
Unit 20
Apex Business Centre
Boscombe Road
Dunstable
Beds LU5 4RL

Many Cultures

Background

This unit can be used to help reinforce the multi-cultural nature of Britain. It does not explore issues of cultural identity but simply highlights the ethnic diversity of Britain. It is also useful as an introduction to topics on the early settlers, emphasising Britain's rich history.

Using the activity sheets

'Our names'

The children are asked to complete the chart by writing down which country or countries each name in the resource is associated with. The following is not comprehensive but may be useful:

Sui/China; Daisy/England; Ruslan/Russia, Eastern Europe; Fatima/ Middle East; Demos/ Cyprus, Greece; Fiona/Scotland; Marvin/ Caribbean, USA; Tara/Ireland; Ade/Africa/ Ravi/ Indian sub-continent; Bronwen/Wales; Ali/ Turkey, Eastern Europe, Indian sub-continent.

The children can also make a chart of the names in their own class. Second names as well as first could be included. Some children will have names from cultures with which they have no connection but this does not matter. The object is to encourage a global view.

'Place names'

While it is possible to work out the meaning of a place name, some are misleading since the meaning may suggest a settlement that did not actually exist, or vice versa. For example Anglo-Saxon villages sometimes adopted Viking names. Prefixes might be from one historical period and suffixes from another. New towns often take names from the past. However, we can point to associations, if not always definitions, and the children may not have realised that place names have origins.

Working with the resource

'British children'

Work through the illustration discussing the children's names. Emphasise that they are all British but they have connections with other countries. You may wish to refer to a world map.

Certain names will apply to more than one culture and you can emphasise this connection.

Useful questions

1. What are the children's names?
2. Do you know anyone with the same name as a child in the picture?
3. Where do you think the children's grandparents might have come from?
4. Have you ever moved home (including within Britain)? What was it like? At this point you could use the picture as an introduction to the Celts, Romans and Anglo-Saxons, asking the children if they know from which countries they originated.

Many Cultures

British children

Ravi

Sui

Ade

Fatima

Ali

Bronwen

Ruslan

Daisy

Marvin

Fiona

Demos

Tara

British children

Our names

All the children in the picture live in Britain. But they also have links with other places.

- Finish the chart below to show this.

Children	Places
Sui	China
Daisy	England
Ruslan	
Fatima	
Demos	
Fiona	
Marvin	
Tara	
Ade	
Ravi	
Bronwen	
Ali	

Many Cultures

Place names

Place names have meanings.

- Read what the words below mean and where they came from.

Celtic word	Meaning
avon	river
loch	lake

Viking word	Meaning
by	farm
thorpe	village

Anglo-Saxon word	Meaning
ford	river crossing
bury	fort
barrow	hill-top

Roman word	Meaning
chester	camp

- Now work out what these names could mean. Write your answers in the 'Meaning' column.

Name	Meaning
Avon	
Chester	
Thorpe	
Westby	
Lochend	
Oxford	
Eastbury	
Barrowby	

8   PRIMARY SPECIALS! *Invaders and Settlers in Britain*   © Folens (copiable page)

The Celts and Romans – The Celtic Way of Life

Teacher's Notes
The unit can be used in conjunction with 'The Roman Way of Life' and 'The Roman Army'.

Background

The Celtic tribes developed in Europe and travelled extensively to parts of Asia Minor, Britain and Ireland. They were a dominant force until the Roman period and had a well-established culture and society. They had a flourishing religion with many nature gods and goddesses, of which Druids were the high priests. The Celts were farmers, traders and craft makers. They grew wheat, barley, beans, flax and herbs, ate wild plants, such as dock leaves, and kept cattle, pigs, sheep and hunting dogs. They were also skilful charioteers and terrifying warriors, reputed to put fear into the hearts of the enemy. Their faces were painted with woad, a blue plant dye, and their hair was probably coated with lime or mud and made spiky. Since they left behind no texts, our written information comes from Roman invaders and may not always be reliable. The name Celt comes from the Greek 'Keltoi'.

Using the activity sheet

'Who were the Celts?'

The children can answer the questions, gain a quick overall picture of Celtic life and refer to it at a later date. The boxes can be filled in with single words or in greater detail according to each child's ability.

Working with the resources

'A Celtic settlement' and 'A Celtic warrior'

Use the illustrations and refer to the Background to discuss Celtic life in sufficient detail for the children to gain a sense of who the Celts were. Although there was a hierarchy of chieftains (male and female), priests, bards and warriors, the land was owned by the tribe not individuals. You can introduce appropriate vocabulary such as 'flax' and 'woad' as you consider suitable.

Useful questions

'A Celtic settlement'
1 What are the buildings like? What do you think are they made from?
2 How is the settlement protected?
3 What did the Celts grow?
4 Where did they store their food, and how?
5 What animals did they keep? Can you guess what they used dogs for?
6 What kind of things did they make?

'A warrior'
1 How can you tell he is a warrior? (He carries weapons and also looks fierce.)
2 What weapons does he have?
3 What is he wearing?
4 Describe his body and face.
5 Describe his hair.
6 Why do you think he looks the way he does?

The Celtic Way of Life

A Celtic settlement

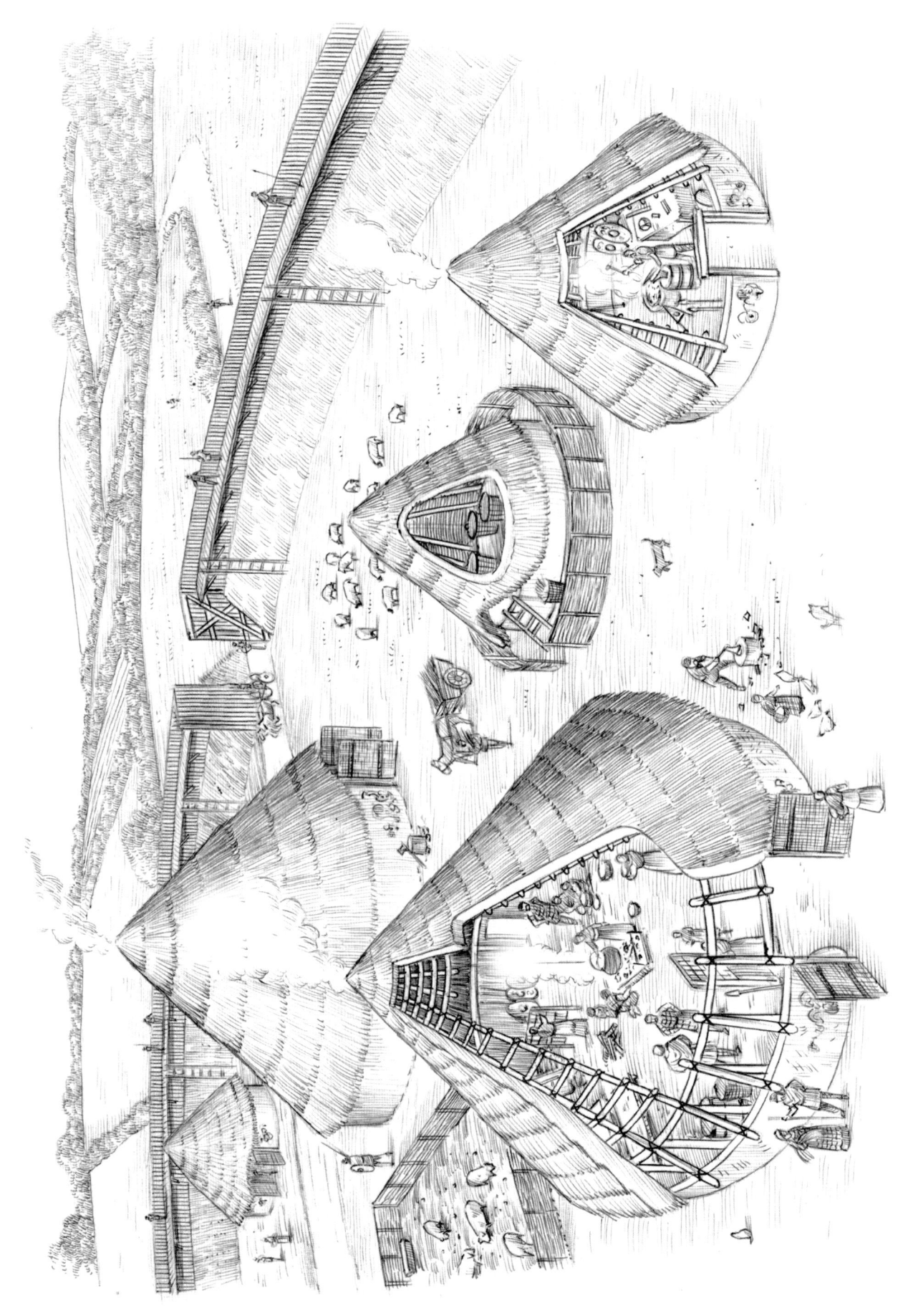

A Celtic settlement

PRIMARY SPECIALS! *Invaders and Settlers in Britain* © Folens (copiable page)

A Celtic warrior

A Celtic warrior

The Celtic Way of Life

Who were the Celts?

- Answer the questions in the boxes.

| What were their houses made from? | How did they protect their farms? |

| What did they grow? | What animals did they keep? |

Who were the Celts?

| What did they make? | What did their warriors look like? |

Celtic Art

Background

Though the Celts made a range of crafts including pots, textiles, wood, bone and leather work, the finest artefacts were in metal. Examples have been found among grave goods, hoards, or as votive offerings left in sacred places for the gods. Special items such as these were made from bronze, gold or occasionally silver, while everyday items were made from iron. Different techniques were used to produce designs, such as hammering sheet metal or chiselling and scratching. Coral and amber were also used for decoration and enamel was produced by melting powdered glass. The torc, a neck ring worn by both men and women, was one of the most important pieces of jewellery. The Celts' love of animal patterns was often displayed in their metalwork and appeared in weapons and jewellery.

Working with the resource

'Celtic designs'

You could ask the children to respond to the illustrations before you provide information. The artefacts are a torc (made from gold, silver and copper), a bronze horse mask, a mirror (made from polished bronze, not glass) and a bronze boar (possibly a helmet crest). They are all representations of artefacts belonging to the British Museum.

Useful questions

1 What are the objects?
2 Can you guess what they were used for?
3 What do you think they are made from?
4 Describe the patterns.
5 Which do you like best? Why?
6 Do you know any other Celtic objects that have decorations on them? (You could refer to the unit, 'The Celtic way of life'.)

Using the activity sheets

'Keep a record'

This is an artefact frame. The children can choose an illustration from 'Celtic designs' and record details about it. It will encourage close observation and should help them to create their own designs and patterns in the Celtic style.

'Be a Celtic artist!'

The brooch shown is similar to a bronze enamelled brooch in a 'dragonesque' design belonging to the British Museum. The decoration can be seen in the frame around the activity sheet, but the children are asked to make up their own for the brooch and colour it in using no more than three colours. It is best if they practice patterns first before they decide what to draw. Encourage them to be guided by the original design. In the centre there appears to be a dragon figure with a head and tail. The diamond pattern suggests scales.

Celtic Art

Celtic designs

Celtic designs

14   PRIMARY SPECIALS! *Invaders and Settlers in Britain*   © Folens (copiable page)

Celtic Art

Keep a record

- Choose an object from 'Celtic designs'.
- Write its name in the middle circle.
- Answer the questions in the surrounding boxes.

What is it for?	**What is it made from?**

What details or patterns does it have?	**How old is it? 50 years? 500 years? Thousands of years?**

© Folens (copiable page)   PRIMARY SPECIALS! *Invaders and Settlers in Britain*

Celtic Art

Be a Celtic artist!

- Look at the brooch below. Can you see that it looks like a dragon?

  The pattern in the middle of the brooch is missing. You can see what it is like by looking at the frame around the drawing on this page.

- Make up your own dragon pattern for the brooch.
- Then colour in the brooch. Use no more than three colours.

A Celtic brooch

Boudicca

Background

Boudicca was the Queen of the Iceni tribe and widow of Prasutagus. Grievances between the Celtic tribes and the Roman colonists came to a head when Boudicca, her daughters, and the Celtic nobles were abused by Roman soldiers. A rebellion ensued around AD60–3 and the Iceni, along with some other tribes, attacked Camulodunum (Colchester). The city, which was poorly defended, was burned to the ground. Successful attacks on Londinium (London) and Verulamium (St Albans) followed. The Celts were finally defeated by Paulinus, the Roman governor, when legionaries, infantry and cavalry were brought from the Rhine. Boudicca, by this time, was dead but how she died remains unclear. Records suggest that she took poison rather than be captured or she became ill and died (which could have occurred from taking poison). She was a fierce warrior, described as intelligent, tall and impressive with a harsh voice and long auburn hair and was extremely able to rally her tribesmen.

Working with the resource

'Boudicca's statue'

The illustrations depict the famous statue of Boudicca with two younger women, probably her daughters. It is shown from two angles. It was made in 1850 by Thomas Thorneycroft, presented to London in 1902 and now stands near the Houses of Parliament. You can use the illustration to point out several things:

- It cannot be a reliable depiction since it was made so long after the event. (For example, Dio Cassius records that Boudicca wore a gold torc.)
- That it tries to capture Boudicca's character or spirit.
- That it shows some features of Celtic life such as the chariot, if inaccurately.

You can also use the illustration as a springboard for telling Boudicca's story.

Useful questions

1 What is Boudicca doing?
2 Where do you think she is going?
3 Who else is with her?
4 What do you think Boudicca was like?
5 About low long ago was the statue made? Is that when Boudicca was alive? About how long ago was she alive?

Using the activity sheets

'Boudicca's fact file'

The children need to select accurate information about Boudicca for the fact file. There is also space to add other facts as required. As a teaching point you might like to follow up with a discussion about information that cannot be verified, such as 'Boudicca's horses were well-treated', so the children can begin to grasp that history does not reveal everything.

'The tribes attack'

Useful words are given to help the children describe the attacking of Colchester, but the children should try to choose their own as well. You could refer to the Roman name Camulodunum if suitable.

Boudicca's statue

Boudicca's statue from the front

Boudicca's statue from the rear

Boudicca's fact file

Underline all the facts that are true about Boudicca (say Boo-dik-ka). Write them in the fact file. (There are four.)

Boudicca was a Celt.	Boudicca was a warrior queen.
The Romans had many gods.	Boudicca's horses were well-treated.
Celtic war paint was blue.	Boudicca's tribe was the Iceni.
Celtic tribes had chariots.	Boudicca fought the Roman army.

Fact file

Boudicca

The tribes attack

Pretend you were living in Colchester when the Celtic tribes attacked. What was it like? Finish the writing frame.

Look! Outside the town walls ...

There are so many, we ...

They wear ...

And have painted ...

Their hair is ...

And they carry ...

They have begun to sweep over the walls and into ...

Will the gods protect us?

Useful words						
Celts	Iceni	killed	cut to pieces	clothes	bodies	faces
wild	fierce	spears	swords	town	homes	

The Roman Army

Background

The Roman soldier had a hard life. As well as taking part in active service, he would be expected to carry out everyday work, such as building roads and maintaining the fort. Those who were craftsmen would be assigned special duties. The centurion was originally in charge of a century – a hundred men, hence the name. This number later dropped to eighty or fewer, though the name remained. The centurion was the equivalent of the non-commissioned officer and often ruled harshly. He was a tough, career soldier.

The Romans invaded and settled in the lowland south and east regions of Britain with few major difficulties, largely because they fought as a cohesive group. Their presence in the highland regions, particularly in the north, was limited to military garrisons. The policy across the Empire was to allow the colonised to run their own affairs but within the Roman structure. Some Celts of higher status, particularly in the towns that adopted the Roman lifestyle, learned Latin and became bilingual. Inter-marriage may also have taken place. However, the ordinary farmers and those in the remote regions retained the Celtic way of life. There were also those who resisted Roman rule, particularly the Druids who had powerful positions in Celtic society as the keepers of knowledge, and who were never totally suppressed.

Working with the resource

'A Roman centurion'

Introduce the illustration of the centurion to the children, explaining how he got his name and what his job involved. He is wearing scale armour and tunic, a helmet with a sideways crest, medals, a cloak, leg guards and Roman sandals and is carrying a sword and a javelin.

Useful questions

1 How can you tell he is a soldier?
2 What weapons does he have?
3 What armour is he wearing?
4 What clothes is he wearing?
5 Do you think he is an ordinary soldier or in charge of other soldiers? Why?
6 What kind of person do you think he is?

Using the activity sheets

'True or false?'

The children will need to recognise and understand the word 'centurion' and 'century' even if they cannot say it correctly. They could try reading the questions to a partner, taking it in turns. The answers are as follows: *True: 2, 3, 5, 8. False: 1, 4, 6, 7.*

'Soldier and warrior'

The children can compare the two illustrations 'A Roman centurion' and 'A Celtic warrior' (see page 11), noting similarities and differences.

The Roman Army

A Roman centurion

A Roman centurion

True or false?

Read the sentences about the Roman centurion.

Tick the ones that are true ✔.

Put a cross by the ones that are not true ✘.

1	Many centurions were women.	
2	A 'century' can mean 'a hundred men'.	
3	A century could be eighty men.	
4	A centurion never went into battle.	
5	The centurion wore a helmet with a sideways crest.	
6	The centurion flew planes.	
7	The centurion wore an animal mask.	
8	A centurion was in charge of a century.	

The Roman Army

Soldier and warrior

- Look at the two pictures 'A Roman centurion' and 'A Celtic warrior'.
  How are they different?
  How are they similar?
- Finish the chart below. The first has been done for you.

Not the same	The same
The Celtic warrior has body paint.	They both carry a sword.

The Roman Way of Life

Teacher's Notes
The unit should be used in conjunction with 'The Celtic Way of Life' for comparison.

Background

Romano-British towns varied in size but the larger ones usually had a forum, with shops, a market and basilica, which was like the town hall and judicial seat. There was also a bathhouse, temples and, sometimes, a theatre. An aqueduct carried the water supply and there were drains and latrines. The town was walled and gated though not heavily defended until later in the Roman period. Some houses might only have a couple of rooms and a workplace, and shops had accommodation above them. The poorest families lived in wooden houses on the outskirts of the town. Larger town houses were more sumptuous. They were 'L' shaped or built around a courtyard with a veranda and had tiled roofs that were fireproof. They were built of flint and mortar, and later of stone.

Working with the resource

'A Roman town'
Use the first illustration to outline the essential features of Roman towns described in 'Background'. You can also discuss the interior of the baths with its mosaics. You may wish to point out that wealthy Romans brought their everyday culture to Britain and that some Celts began to adopt the Roman way of life.

Useful questions

1 What do you think the picture shows?
2 Can you find the market place? What was it for?
3 What other buildings are in the market place? Do you know what they are for? (See the two-storey basilica or town hall and courts.)
4 Can you find the bath house? What was this for?
5 How does water reach the town? (By way of the aqueduct.)
6 What is surrounding the town? How do people get in?
7 What other buildings can you see? (Temple, shops, homes.)

Using the activity sheets

'Making a mosaic'
Roman mosaics could include figures or be based on geometric designs such as the one depicted here. If you prefer, the children can use glossy magazines cut into squares instead of sticky paper to create the mosaic. They should try to preserve the pattern's shape, by choosing different colours but keeping to the same colour for each section.

'Romans and Celts'
The children will need the resource 'A Celtic settlement' from the unit 'The Celtic Way of Life', as well 'A Roman town'. They can make direct comparisons, for example, between the building style and how the different settlements were defended. The children can add more points as needed. Try to encourage them to see the Celts as different from the Romans rather than unsophisticated. Point to the exceptional quality of Celtic artwork.

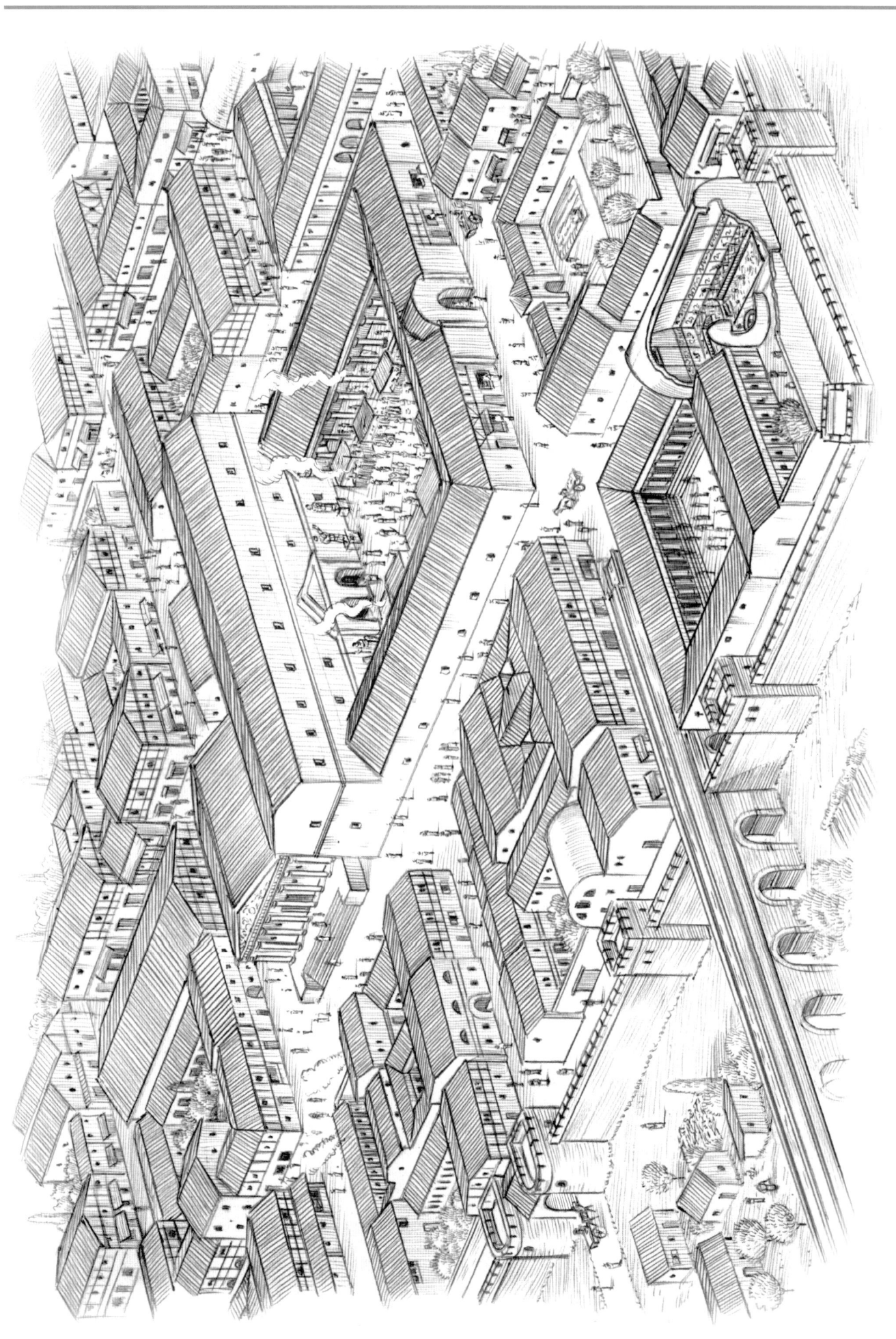

The Roman Way of Life

A Roman town

A Roman town

The Roman Way of Life

Making a mosaic

- Turn the pattern below into a Roman mosaic.
- Choose the colours you will use for each section.
- Cut different coloured sticky paper into small squares and stick them on. Remember to cover the whole pattern.

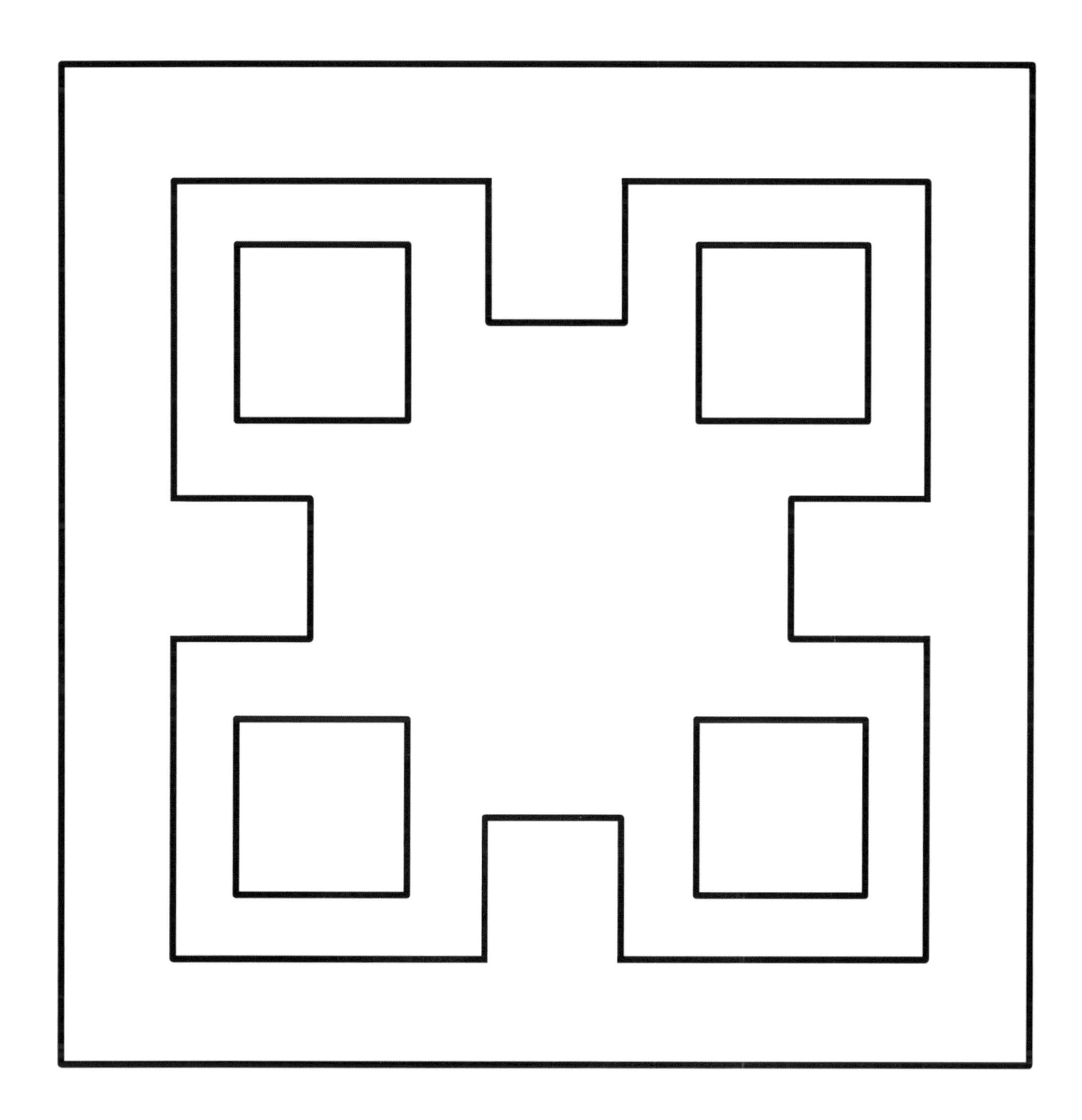

The Roman Way of Life

Romans and Celts

Look at the pictures 'A Celtic settlement' and 'A Roman town'.
Fill in the chart to show the differences between them.

	Roman town	**Celtic settlement**
1		
2		
3		
4		
5		
6		
7		
8		
9		
10		

The Villa

Background

In Britain the villa was situated outside the town and was set in an estate. It was often owned by wealthy Britons who had adopted the Roman way of life. The land was worked, grain and other produce grown, and, in some cases, there were metal workshops and potteries. Some villas seem to have developed from Celtic farms eventually becoming Roman in style. Built around a courtyard or courtyards, the interiors would have mosaics, frescoes, painted walls and tiled floors. There was usually an under-floor heating system (a hypocaust) and bronze oil lamps would provide light. There would also be a bath-house. The kitchen would have a stove, fuelled by charcoal or wood with a charcoal pit on top. Wooden shelves would hold utensils, such as a pestle and mortar with grit embedded in it for grinding seeds, nuts and herbs. The vast majority of people in Roman Britain would eat bread, gruel, fruit and vegetables. In the villas a meal could involve several courses and would include foods such as chestnuts, walnuts and figs, which had recently been introduced into Britain.

Using the activity sheet

'Boiled eggs, Roman style'

The children should search for the number cues to sequence the recipe in the following order: *First, Next day, Third, Fourth, Fifth, Last of all.*

Working with the resources

'The dining room' and 'The kitchen'

The first illustration shows a dining room belonging to a wealthy Romano-Briton where guests would also be entertained. It has a mosaic floor and brightly patterned walls. There are only a few pieces of furniture, including a Roman couch.

The kitchen, in the second illustration, has a charcoal stove, table for preparing food, shelves for storage and amphorae for holding wine. The larder contains a wide range of foods. The foods are fish, duck, rabbit, eggs, herbs, bread, tomatoes, cucumbers, oysters, mussels, olives, corn, walnuts, grapes, figs and cherries.

Useful questions

'The dining room'

1 Can you guess what kind of room this was?
2 How is the room decorated?
3 How is the room different from your rooms at home? How is it similar?
4 Would you like to live in this kind of room? Why?

'The kitchen'

1 How is the food cooked? What makes the heat?
2 Where would the cook prepare the food?
3 What kind of food did wealthy Romans eat?
4 Where do you think the wine was stored?
5 How is it different from your kitchen at home?
6 What kinds of equipment do we have that the Romans didn't?

The Villa

The dining room

The dining room

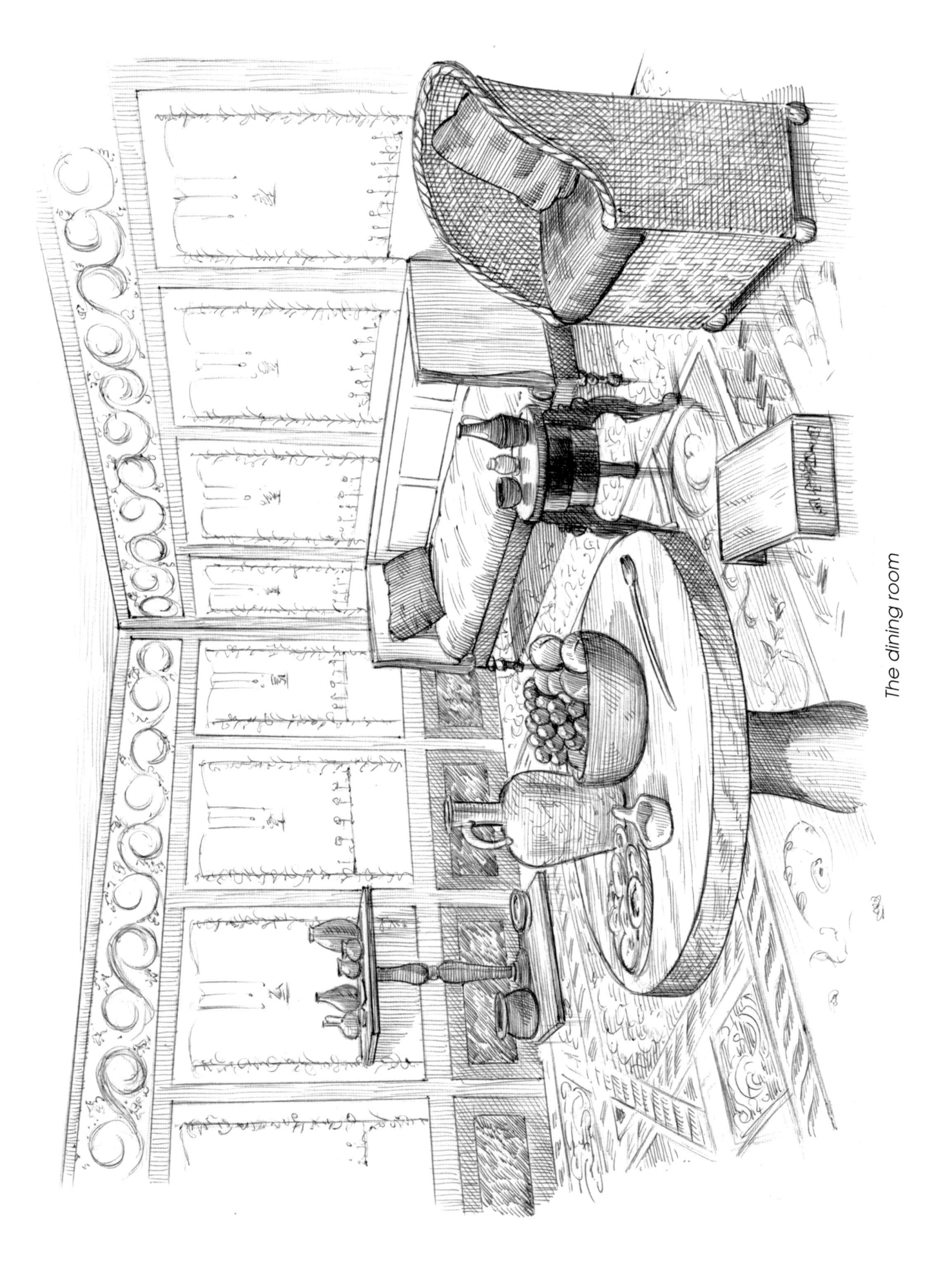

30   PRIMARY SPECIALS! *Invaders and Settlers in Britain*   © Folens (copiable page)

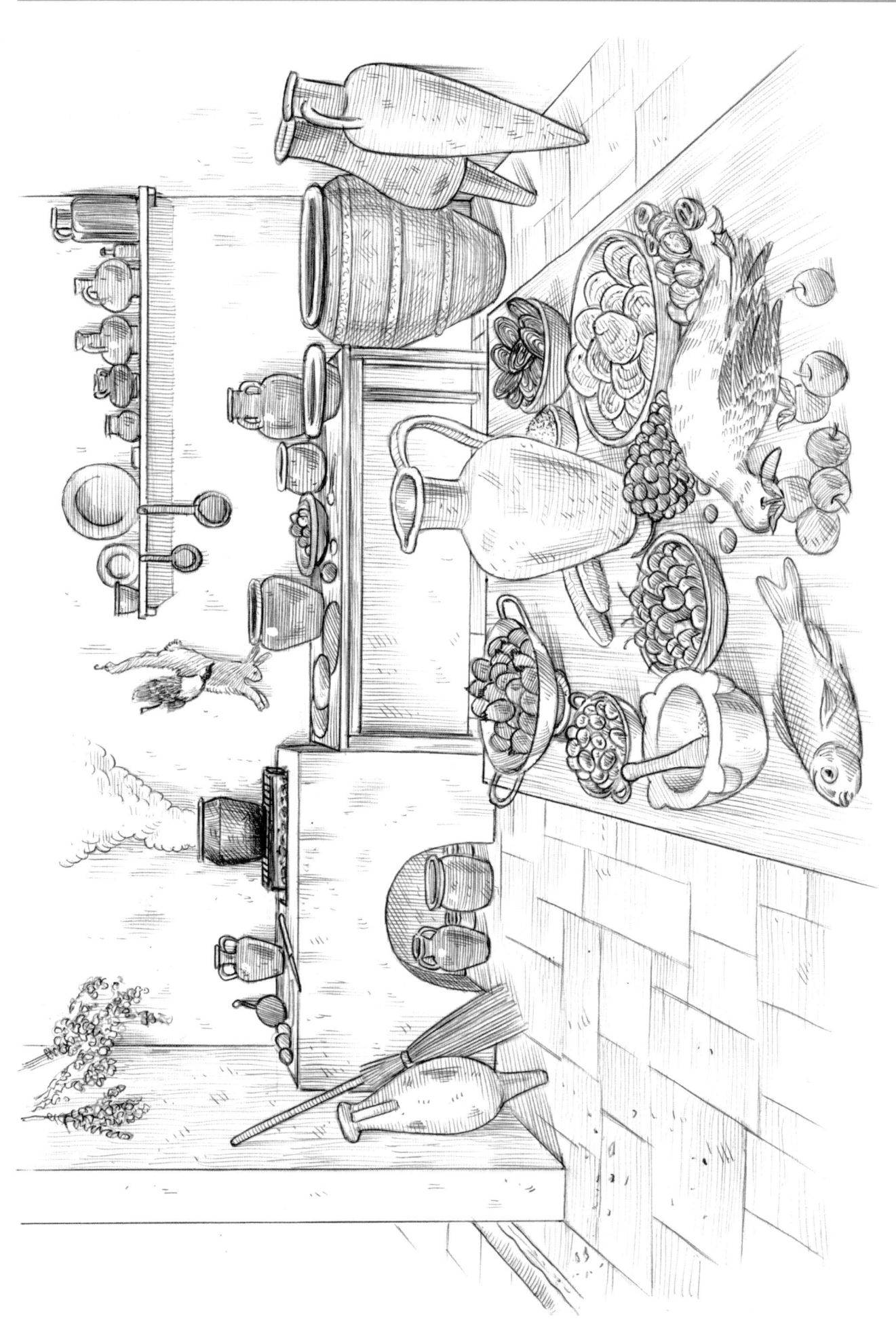

The kitchen

The Villa

The kitchen

The Villa

Boiled eggs, Roman style

The Romans had many recipes. They often used a fish sauce called liquamen. This was like adding salt.

Number the recipe for boiled eggs, Roman style, in the correct order. The first has been done for you.

Next day boil four eggs and remove the shells.

Third, mix the pine kernels with a little honey.

1   First, soak 25g of pine kernels overnight.

Fourth, add a little vinegar.

Fifth, add a little liquamen.

Last of all, pour the mixture over the eggs.

The Anglo-Saxons – The Sutton Hoo Burial

Background

In 1939 excavations into a series of burial mounds, or barrows, at Sutton Hoo revealed the imprint of a Saxon burial ship along with a magnificent collection of grave goods, the most important discovered to date in Britain and Europe. The work was led by Basil Brown, and further excavations have been carried out since. The ship itself had disintegrated but the sandy soil had been stained where it had stood and the rivets were left. Archaeologists were able to gain a clear picture of what the ship must have looked like. It was built with overlapping planks (clinker built) and was probably dragged to the trench on rollers. The body (which was never found) would have been placed with the grave goods in the burial chamber built in the middle of the ship. The whole area would then have been covered over to form a mound.

Working with the resource

'The buried ship'

It is best to begin by explaining to the children where Sutton Hoo is and what it is famous for. You may wish to refer to a map. Explain also that Sutton Hoo is the site of a series of mounds that are being excavated and that have been disturbed in the distant past and sometimes robbed.

The artist's illustration clearly shows the impression left by the ship. The children can try to guess what it is and how it might have arrived there. Discuss the term 'archaeology' with them. If you wish to pursue this further see the 'The Archaeological Dig' unit in *Primary Specials! Ancient Egypt*. This describes the job of the archaeologist and also looks at the way in which fragments of artefacts are found and later pieced together.

Using the activity sheets

'Sutton Hoo'

The children can use the spidergram to record essential details about Sutton Hoo. They are also asked to say what they would like to know about the ship. If feasible they could carry out a search in the library or on the Internet with your guidance.

'Our talk'

This writing frame allows the children to record exploratory talk. They can write down what was discussed about the burial ship and, perhaps, how it came to be buried at Sutton Hoo. You can also use the frame for other topics and modify the starter sentences if you wish.

Useful questions

1. What do you think the picture shows? What object was once buried there?
2. Who do you think the people are? (Mrs Edith Pretty, who owned the land and invited archaeologists to investigate, is also included.) What are the people doing?
3. The object that was once there was a ship. It was buried around one thousand four hundred years ago. How do you think it got there, away from the river?

The Sutton Hoo Burial

The buried ship

The buried ship

The Sutton Hoo Burial

Sutton Hoo

Fill in the boxes.

What is Sutton Hoo?	**Where is Sutton Hoo?**

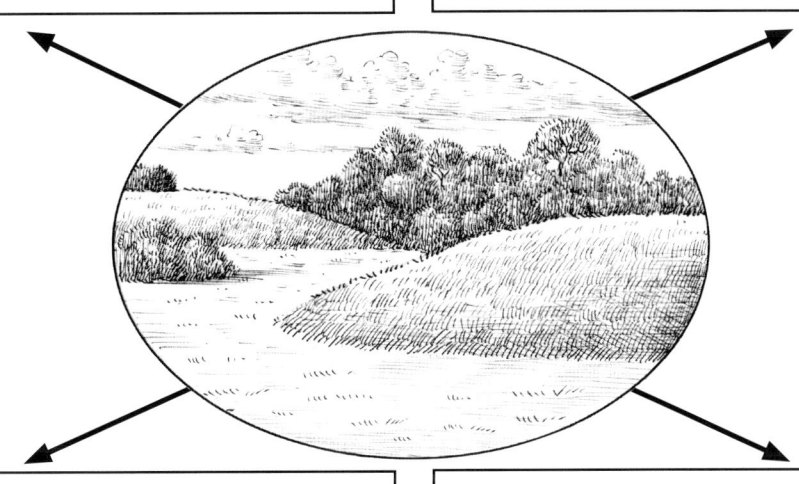

Why is Sutton Hoo so famous?	**What does a ship-burial mean?**

What else would you like to know about the ship?

I would like to know …

The Sutton Hoo Burial

Our talk

Finish the writing frame.

> In our group we talked about …
>
> The teacher said that …
>
> And asked us …
>
> One person said that …
>
> Another said that …
>
> I said …
>
> After thinking about it, I finally thought that …

The Sutton Hoo Treasure

Background

The grave goods found in the burial chamber at Sutton Hoo included parts of a helmet and shield, a sword and scabbard, drinking horns and a set of silver bowls, among many other artefacts. These are beautifully decorated, sometimes in gold, with garnets and millefiori glass (which is like enamel). A lyre was also found; it is made from wood and decorated with gold, garnets and animal designs. It was probably used to accompany storytelling. One of the most interesting and mysterious objects found is the Whetstone-Sceptre. This is too elaborate to have been used for sharpening tools and was most likely used for ceremonial purposes. If it is a symbol of sovereignty this would suggest the burial was of a king or noble. The stone itself was found separated from the iron ring and bronze stag, which were all later reassembled. It has been suggested that the whetstone represents the 'sharpener of swords' (the king would have given swords to those nobles who had supported him) while the stag represents speed and courage. The Whetstone-Sceptre, the lyre and other Sutton Hoo treasures can be seen in the British Museum, where this information comes from.

Working with the resources

'The Whetstone-Sceptre' and 'The lyre'

You could discuss with the children details about the whetstone and the lyre by referring to 'Background'. Explain the whetstone's association with royalty and how it might give clues about who was buried in the chamber.

Useful questions

1 Have you any idea what the object could be? Try guessing.
2 What materials do you think it is made from?
3 Describe the patterns.
4 When would you use the object?
5 Who do you think would own something like this?

Using the activity sheet

'Grave goods'

This artefact frame is harder then 'Keep a record' in the unit, 'Celtic Art', which you could use instead if you prefer. For example, here the children are asked to estimate how long ago the artefact was found. The children should record details about either the lyre or the Whetstone-Sceptre in the boxes. Useful words are given to help them. They can also write additional information as you see fit.

The Sutton Hoo Treasure

The Whetstone-Sceptre

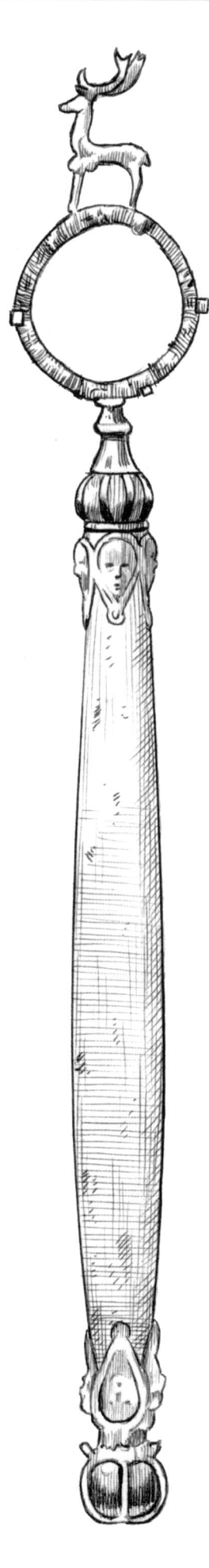

The Whetstone-Sceptre

The lyre

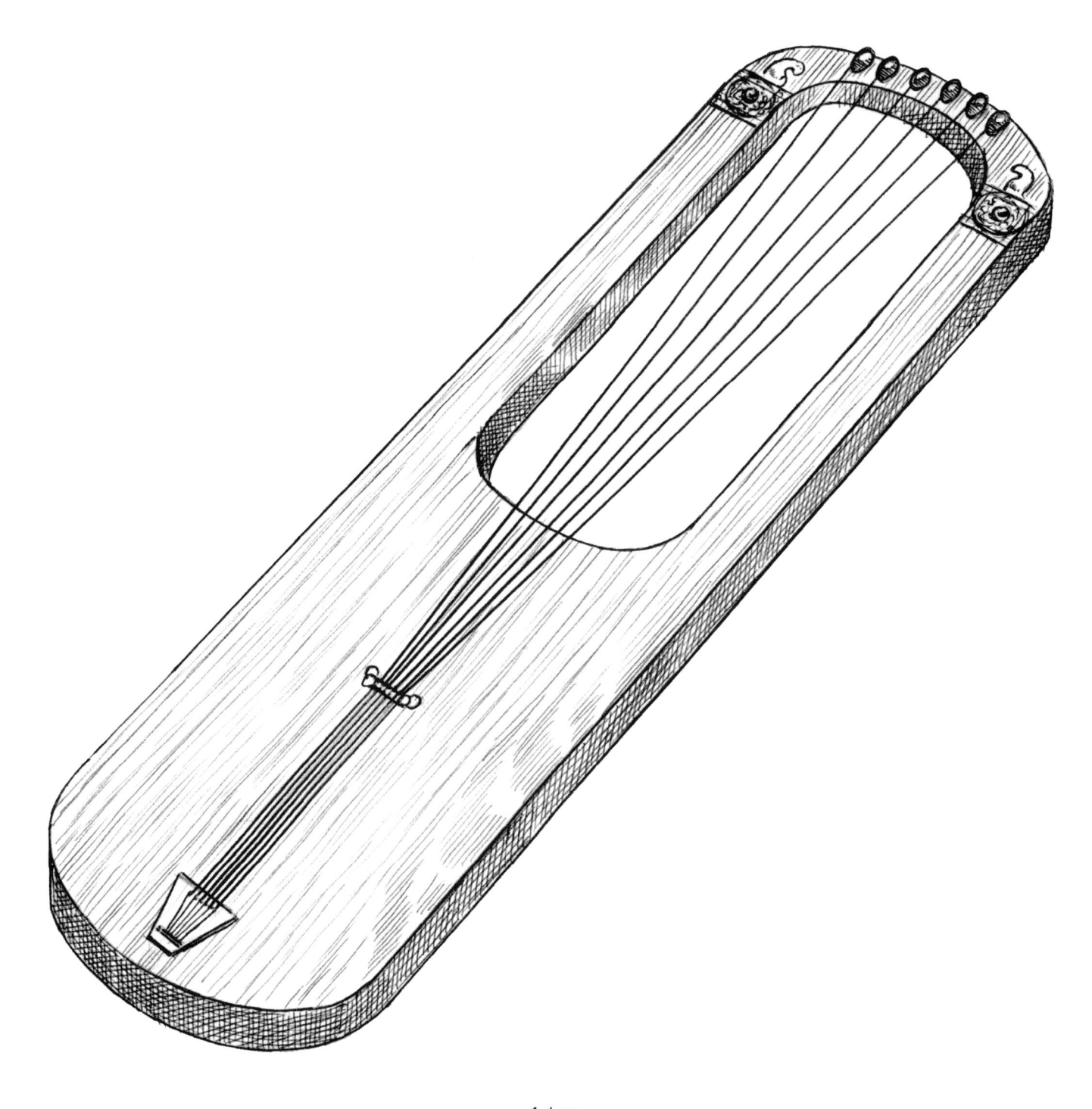

A lyre

The Sutton Hoo Treasure

Grave goods

Choose the lyre or the Whetstone-Sceptre. Write its name in the middle box and answer the following questions about it. Fill in the boxes.

How long ago was it found?		**Where was it found?**
What is it made from?		**When was it used?**
Who would own it?		**What decoration has it got?**

Choose from these words to help you.

> Sutton Hoo   music   storytelling   wood   gold   garnets
> stone   stag   bronze   iron   special times
> royal   king   queen

The East Anglian King

Background

The ship burial chamber at Sutton Hoo probably belongs to Redwald, king of East Anglia. He was in power from the late sixth century until the early seventh and is mentioned by Bede, a monk and scholar who recorded the period in *The Ecclesiastical History of the English People*. Redwald was an important monarch at a time when intrigue and conspiracy were rife and when the power of the kings fluctuated. He appears to have been instrumental in assisting Edwin regain power in Northumbria and in refusing help to Ethelfrith in his bid to have Edwin put to death. Sources also reveal that Redwald adopted Christianity, while at the court of the king of Kent, but on returning to East Anglia was persuaded by his wife to reject it. He seems however, to have kept his options open and had a Christian altar built alongside a pagan one. If true, the tale gives us a small insight into Redwald's personality. But, more importantly, it illustrates that the country was going through a period of profound change, which would culminate in the adoption of Christianity as the established religion and the decline of the ancient pagan beliefs.

Working with the resource

'Redwald'

Information is given about Redwald that the children should try to read on their own or in pairs. Key words are in bold so that you could discuss the meanings if you need to.

Useful questions

1 Who is Redwald? Where did he come from?
2 How long ago did he live?
3 Why do people think he might have been in the grave at Sutton Hoo?
4 What was Redwald's religion?
5 What do you think Redwald was like? Why?

Using the activity sheets

'Who was Redwald?'

The children are asked to identify the information by ticking the correct boxes. The statements relate to each of the paragraphs in the resource and they follow these in order, so if a child is unsure of the answer he or she can check. You might like to encourage them to tick the paragraphs off as they go. At the end they are asked to explain to a partner what some of the key words mean. They could take it in turns to do this.

'Who was in the grave?'

This writing frame should help the children to pull together the information they have gathered about who was buried in the grave. Useful words are supplied, but the children should try to use their own as well.

The East Anglian King

Redwald

No one really knows who was buried in the ship at **Sutton Hoo**. A body was not found. But there are clues.

For example, there were lots of **grave goods**. Can you remember what grave goods are? They are objects found in the grave. The ones in the ship were very beautiful. So they must have belonged to someone important.

Many people think it was a **warrior king**. They think it was **Redwald**. He was king of **East Anglia**. This lies along the east coast of Britain. If you look on a map you can find where it is.

We know a few things about Redwald. We know he worshipped **nature gods**. Thor, the god of Thunder, was one of these. Lots of people worshipped nature gods at the time. We also know that Redwald became a **Christian**. But then he appears to have changed his mind. He may have worshipped both.

Another thing we know is that he was asked to murder a king called Edwin. But he refused. Instead he helped **Edwin** get back in power.

We think Redwald was living about **1400 years ago**. If he is the king buried at Sutton Hoo it is a very important find.

Who was Redwald?

- Read the following sentences.
- Tick the boxes beside the sentences that are true.
- Put a cross beside those that are not true.

	True	Not true
There was no body found in the ship buried at Sutton Hoo.	☐	☐
There were no objects found in the ship.	☐	☐
Most people think a warrior king was buried there.	☐	☐
Redwald was a Christian and he believed in nature gods.	☐	☐
Edwin was Redwald's enemy.	☐	☐
Redwald lived about fifty years ago.	☐	☐

- What do these key words mean? Tell a partner.

Sutton Hoo   **grave goods**   **warrior king**   **nature gods**

The East Anglian King

Who was in the grave?

Finish the writing frame. Read it through before you begin.

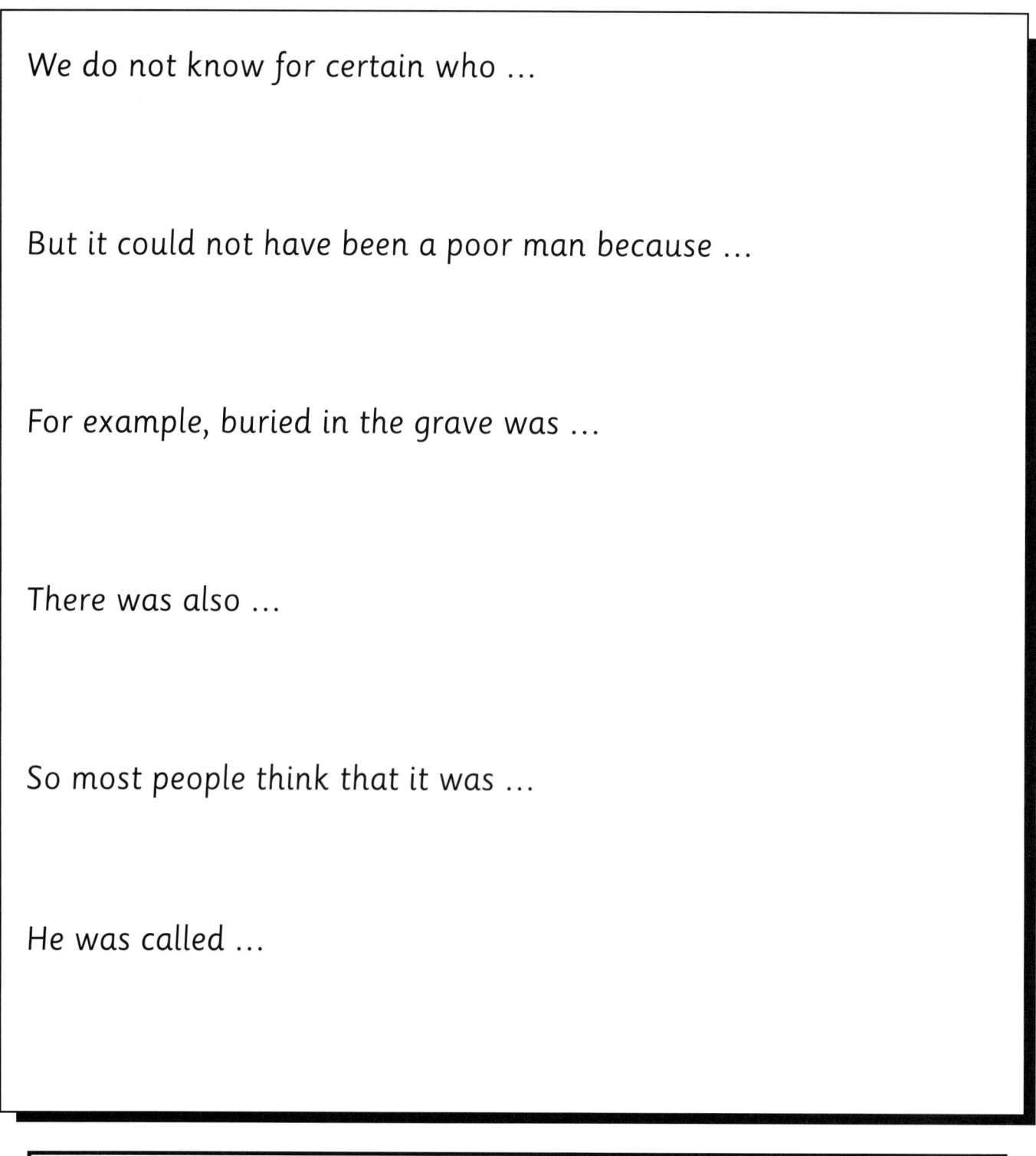

We do not know for certain who …

But it could not have been a poor man because …

For example, buried in the grave was …

There was also …

So most people think that it was …

He was called …

Useful words

burial chamber   helmet   sword   sceptre   lyre   gold

silver bowls   jewels   rich   king   Redwald

King of East Anglia   warrior king

Beowulf

Background

The epic poem, 'Beowulf', is thought to date from around the eighth century. Beowulf is the Norse hero who slays the monster Grendel and its mother. The poem also tells of his death as an aged warrior. Its origins are obscure but certain references, for example to Beowulf's uncle, Hygelac, seem to have a basis in recorded history and the poem may include factual incidents as well as fictional ones. In any case, its great value historically lies in the insight it gives us into the period. It illustrates the value placed on the warrior hero and makes reference to earlier tales, suggesting a storytelling tradition. The writing is vivid and powerful and still able to captivate audiences. The most recent translation is by Seamus Heaney (1999, Faber).

Using the activity sheet

'What next?'

The children can record ideas from the discussion above, anticipating what might happen in the story. They could work in pairs to talk about further ideas. The page is organised to encourage one idea to lead on to another and the children can keep asking the question, 'And then?' to build up a series of events.

Working with the resource

'Out of the marshlands'

This extract comes from *Beowulf and the Monster* by Brian Patten, (published by Scholastic, 1999) and describes how Grendel and his mother are slain. Brian Patten's rewriting of the story for children, in its mood, pace and choice of language, captures the spirit of the original.

You will need to read the extract to the children but they can follow it with you and some may be able to join in. Discuss the story with them. The following questions focus on mood and genre and how the story might develop.

Useful questions

1. How did the story make you feel?
2. Have you read any similar stories? What kind of stories does it remind you of? Why?
3. Roughly how long ago do you think it was first written?
4. What do you think will happen next in the story? Think of more than one possibility.

Beowulf

Out of the marshlands

Grendel the monster has crept out from the marshlands and attacked the Great Hall.

After a century without the taste of human blood, that taste was as fresh and sweet as blackberries to Grendel. He came back again and again. Night after night he returned to the village, searching the surrounding houses for unwary humans. And each night he sat brooding in the Great Hall like a bloated spider inside its web.

Soon no one dared to sleep in their homes. People would only visit the village in the daylight when they were sure Grendel would not come. And as for the Great Hall, they shunned it both day and night.

The Great Hall, their pride and joy, stood empty. Darkness fell upon it. Owls colonized its rafters and rats scurried about its floor.

It was the greatest disaster that had ever befallen the king and his people. At night they all hid in the forest like animals and whenever Grendel found a careless sleeper, he would drag them to the Great Hall and devour them.

There was no laughter in the kingdom. No songs. No feasting. No joy. Stories of the monster's terrible deeds spread far and wide. Warriors came from distant lands, all hoping to prove themselves heroes and destroy Grendel, but none was quite great enough.

The first warrior to come had a magic bow.

'I'm the greatest warrior of all,' he said. 'I will destroy Grendel with my bow.'

The king hoped against hope that the stranger could fulfil his boast. At dusk when Grendel rose up from his nest of rats' bones and came to the village, the warrior took out a magic arrow and aimed it at Grendel's heart. But the arrow might as well have been a feather for all the harm it did.

Out of the marshlands (continued)

The next warrior to come had a magic dagger. It might as well have been a reed for all the harm it did.

Other warriors came, and many lost their lives. Some were boastful fools and others were brave. All the same, none could defeat Grendel who merely taunted them with his terrible song:

> "Sweet human meat's the best to eat,
> And human bones the best to grind.
> Human blood will flow again
> And cold terror haunt the human mind."

And so the years passed and the dust lay as thick as snow in the Great Hall. People's spirits were broken and no one took pride in themselves or their land. Crops failed in the fields. Houses fell to rack and ruin. Paths became overgrown and were forgotten. Warriors had long since ceased to come and pit their strength against Grendel. More human bones than rats' bones littered his nest now.

Then early one frosty morning as winter took hold of the kingdom, a boat was seen sailing over the horizon …

From *Beowulf and the Monster* by Brian Patten

Beowulf

What next?

1 What do you think happens in the story next?

2 Think of three ideas and where they could lead.

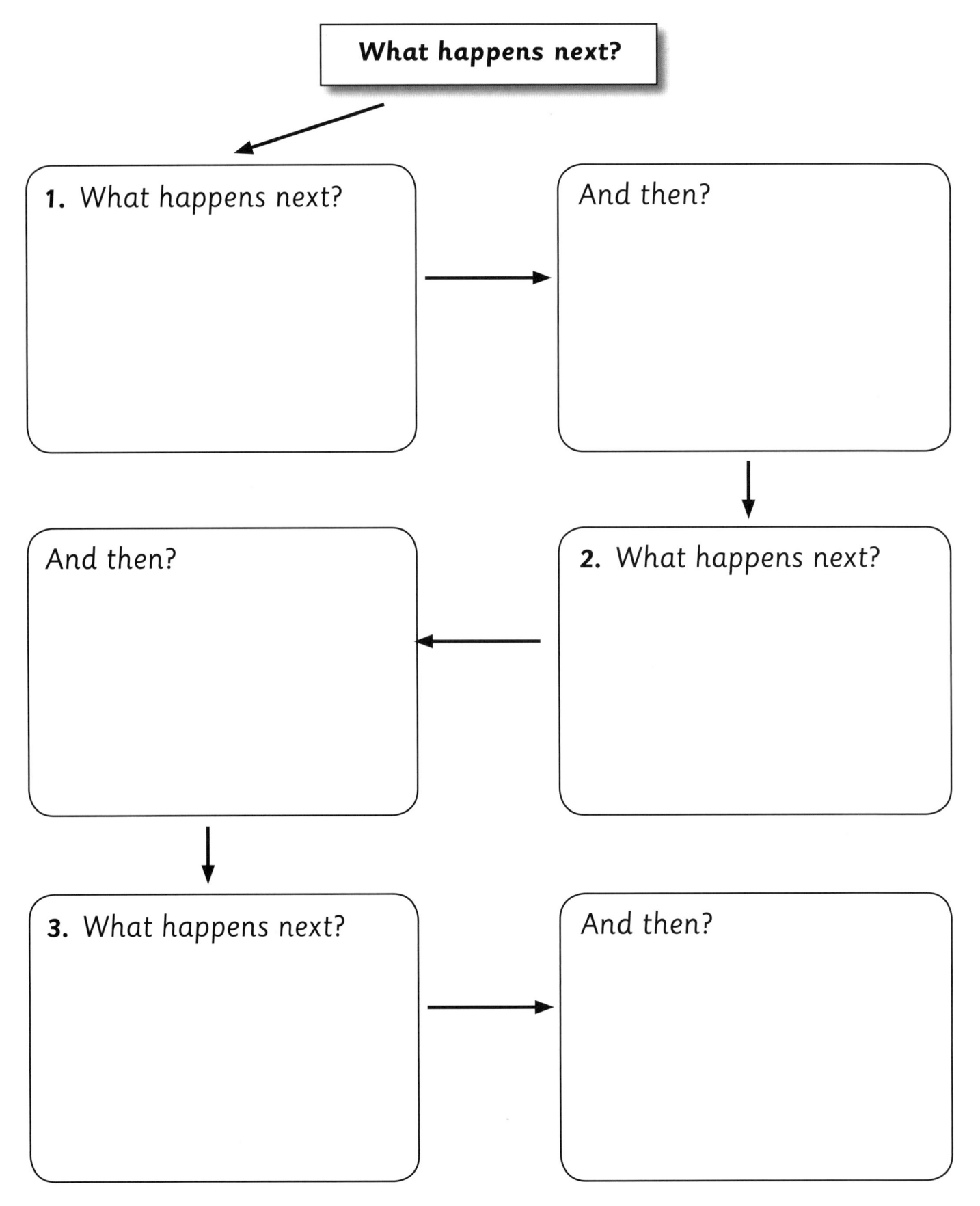

What happens next?

1. What happens next?

And then?

And then?

2. What happens next?

3. What happens next?

And then?

The Vikings –
Who were the Vikings?

Background

From around the eighth century the Vikings, who inhabited Denmark, Norway and Sweden, began to make lengthy voyages in search of greater wealth and lands. Lack of resources or over-population have been suggested as reasons, but no one is quite sure why. Those from Sweden sailed across the Baltic Sea and made successful forays into Russia and Eastern Europe, travelling into the interior. The Danish and Norwegian Vikings sailed west to parts of Greenland, Iceland, North America, including Newfoundland (Vinland), the Faeroe Islands, and Northern France. They invaded and settled the Orkneys and Shetlands, swept round to Ireland and along the east coast of Britain. One of the first recorded raids was in 793 on Lindisfarne (Holy Island) off the coast of Northumbria. However, the Vikings were skilful traders as well as warriors and were able to barter and negotiate. They traded goods made from their own local resources and also goods traded or stolen from other countries.

Using the activity sheet

'The key'

Here the children have to match the symbols to the names to complete the key. They can refer back to the maps to remind themselves of the resources and goods available through trading.

Working with the resources

'Viking homelands' and 'Viking voyages'

The two maps can be used together and you may wish also to use a world map to show the children where the Scandinavian countries are in relation to the rest of the world, including Britain and Ireland. Discuss with them what trading and bartering mean before beginning, perhaps by pointing to the way that they swap goods with each other.

Useful questions

'Viking homelands'

1. Where did the Vikings live?
2. Look carefully at the coast of Norway, Denmark and Sweden. How would you describe it? (Explain to the children what fjords are and how the Vikings designed their boats to travel along them.)
3. Can you guess what kind of things the Vikings traded by looking at the map? What would they be used for? (You will need to explain what some symbols are and what they mean, such as 'amber'.)

'Viking voyages'

1. Do you know what countries are on this map?
2. Look at the routes. Where did the Vikings go when they travelled west? (You might like to point to the compass here.)
3. What kind of things did the Vikings find in Britain and Ireland?

Who Were the Vikings?

Viking homelands

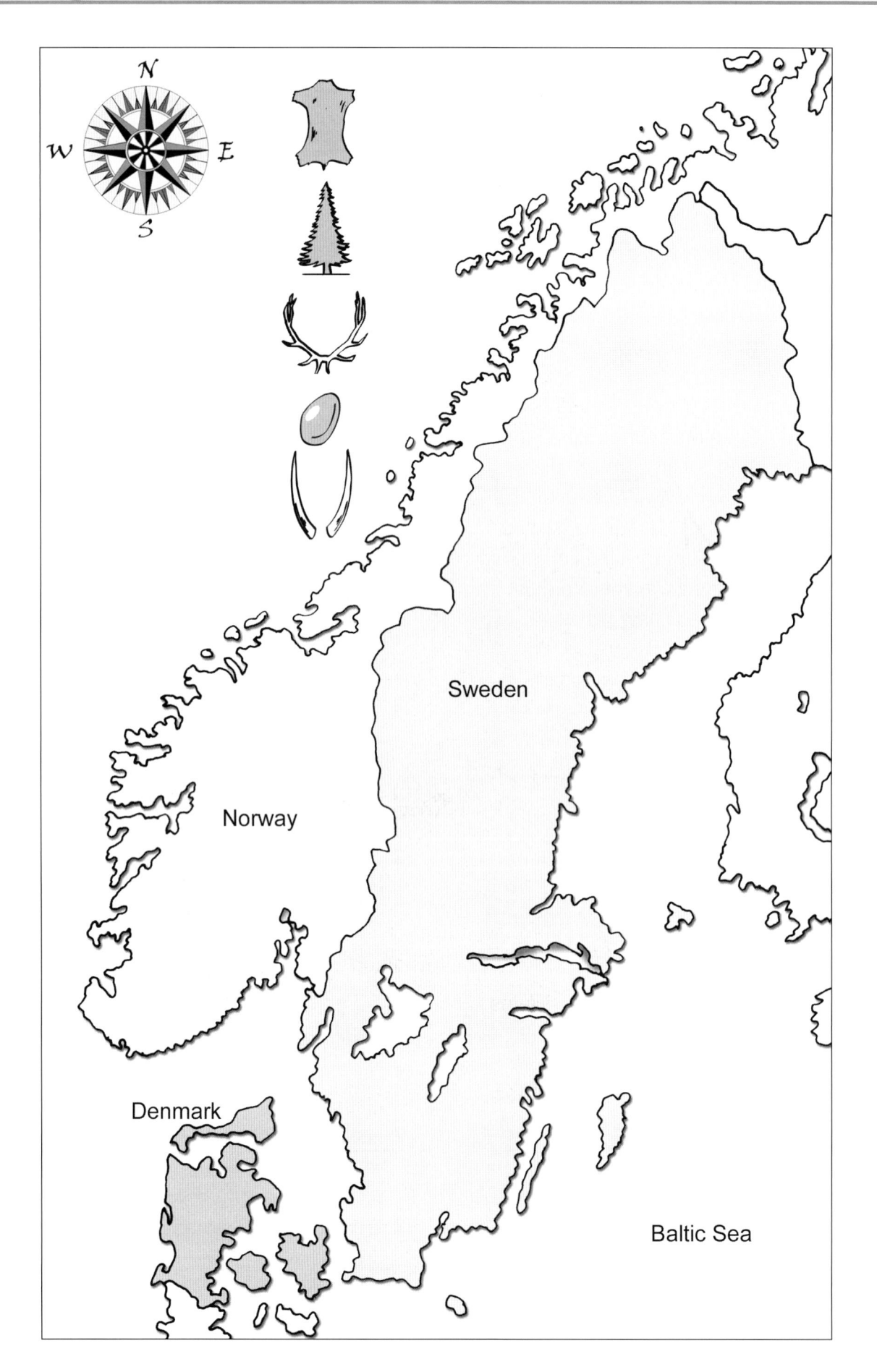

Viking homelands

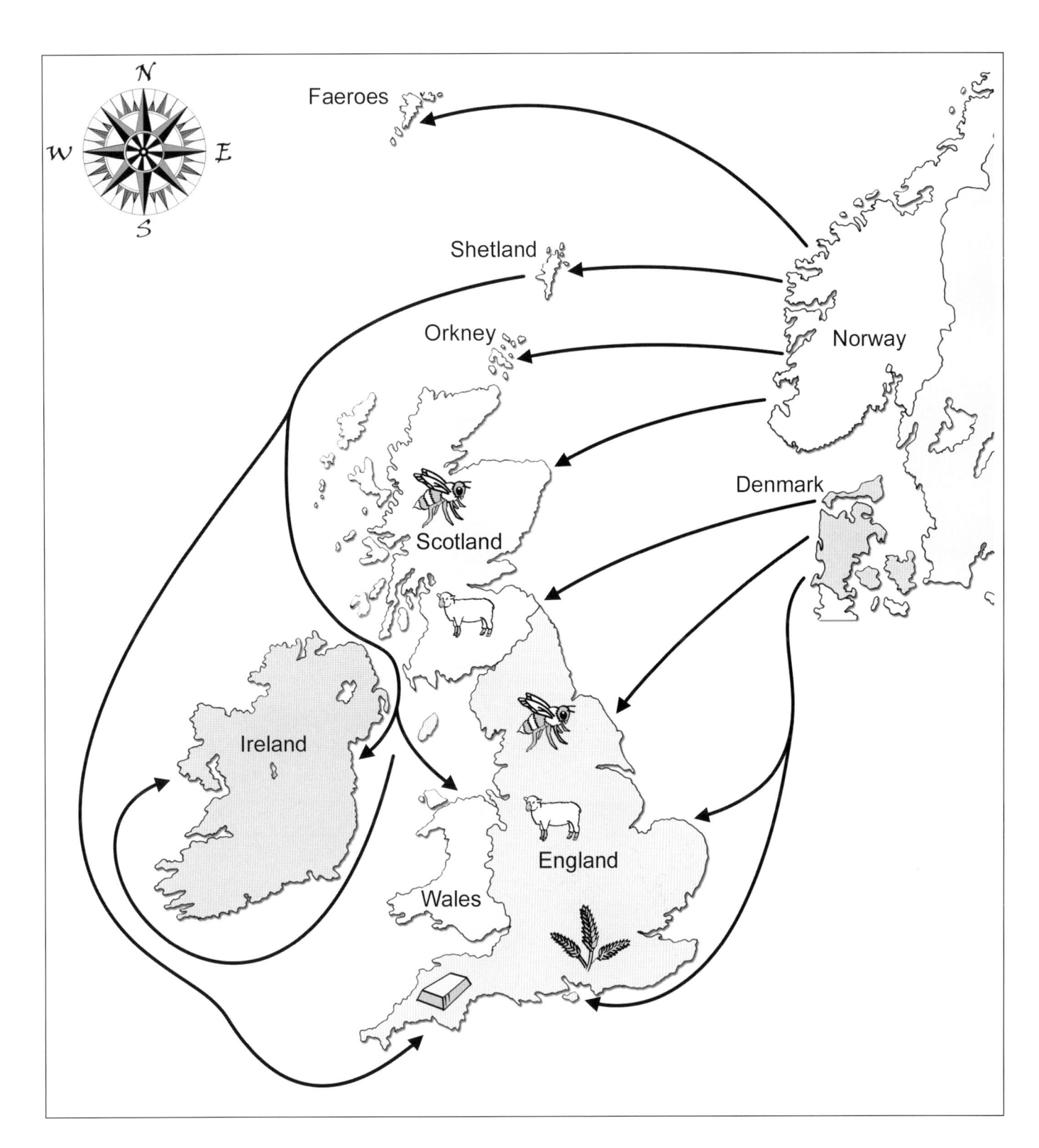

Viking voyages

Who Were the Vikings?

Viking voyages

Who Were the Vikings?

The key

Here are some goods that the Vikings traded from their own countries, on the first map – 'Viking homelands':

animal skins, walrus tusks, wood, amber, antlers.

Here are some they found in the countries on the second map 'Viking voyages':

wheat, sheep, tin, honey.

Write the names next to the correct picture in the key below.

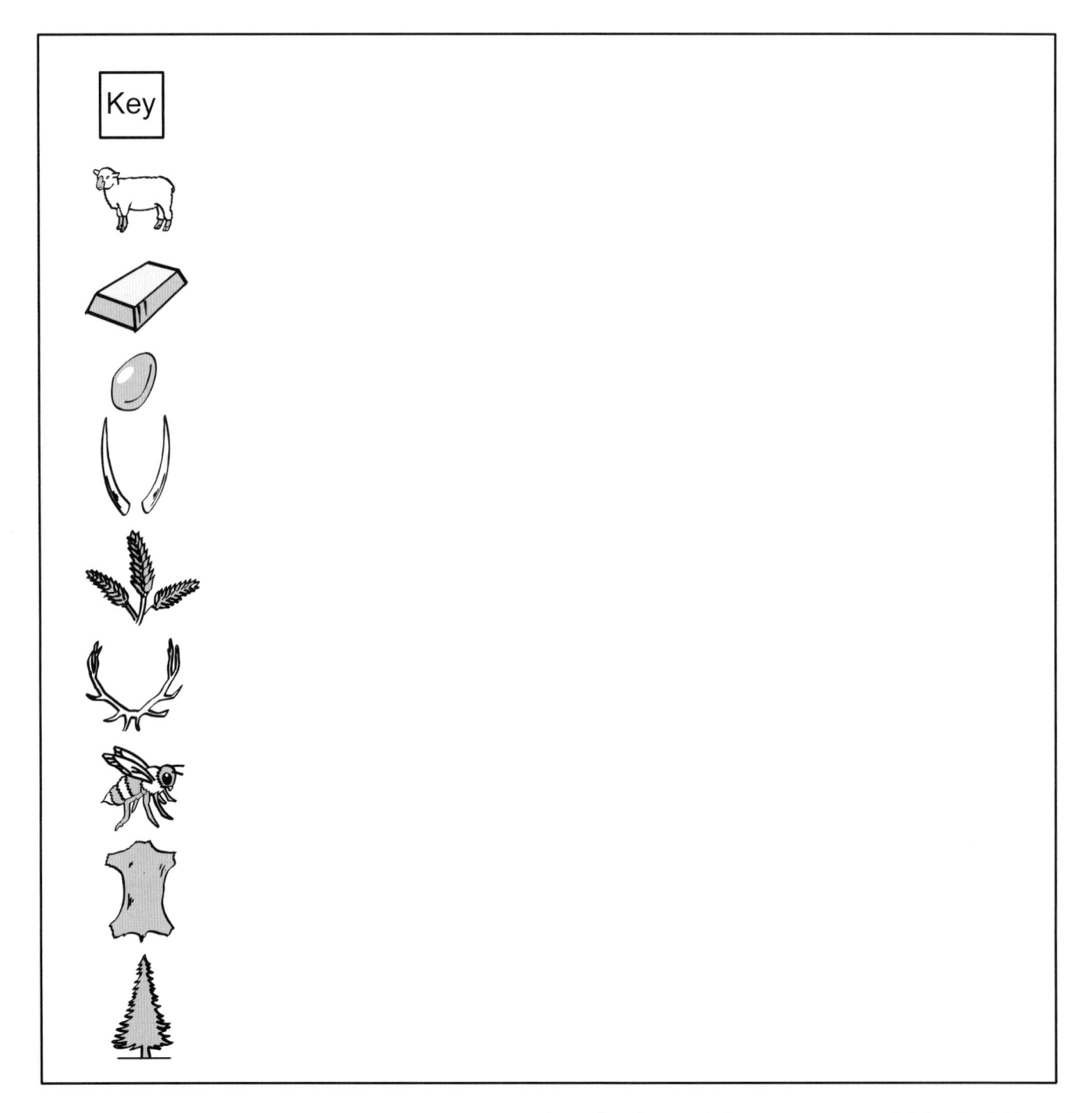

The Viking Longship 1

Teacher's Notes
This and the following unit are designed to be used together.

Background

The Vikings' success owes much to their ship-building skills. The best-known vessel, the longship, was made from oak and built to be particularly flexible, so that it could withstand rough weather. In addition, the keel (the strip of wood running from length to length along the bottom of the ship) jutted out, giving extra stability. There was a large, heavy steering oar and also a sail, which was often dyed, sometimes in stripes or geometric patterns. The slim longship was fast-moving on the open seas. It was large enough to carry provisions and shelter and was also highly adaptable and could sail up narrow inlets and rivers, a point discussed in the next unit.

Using the activity sheets

'Sails and oars'
The children can complete the ship by adding the features outlined. Encourage them to draw the features without looking at the illustration first, and then make it available as necessary. You can note how much they recall.

'Memory work'
This task also helps to reinforce the features of the Viking longship. The children will have met the vocabulary in the previous discussion. If you wish to see whether they have retained the meanings over a period of time, you could use the activity sheet at a later date, when the next unit is completed for example.

Working with the resource

'On the open sea'
The illustration shows the longship on the open sea with sails full. You can refer to 'Background' and the construction of the ship and encourage the children to think about how the ship was driven. The prow is carved with a circular decoration, similar to the Oseberg ship which was excavated in 1904 from a burial mound in Norway. Larger warships often had dragon prows. Introduce vocabulary such as: longship, voyage, prow, keel, sail, mast, oars, steering oar and trunk. (See the activity sheet, 'Memory work' for guidance.)

Useful questions

1. Why do you think the ship was called a longship?
2. How do you think it was driven?
3. Why do you think it could move quickly? (Shape as well as the sail helped with speed.)
4. What do you think the oar at the back of the ship was for?
5. What do you think the 'tent' is for?
6. Describe the decoration on the prow.
7. What are the Vikings sitting on? (Personal goods were kept in chests, which the Vikings also used as seats, usually when rowing the ship.)
8. How is the ship different from ships we have today?

The Viking Longship 1

On the open sea

On the open sea

Sails and oars

Below is an outline of a Viking longship.
Draw these things on the ship: sail, oars, shelter, steering oar and holes for the oars.

A Viking longship

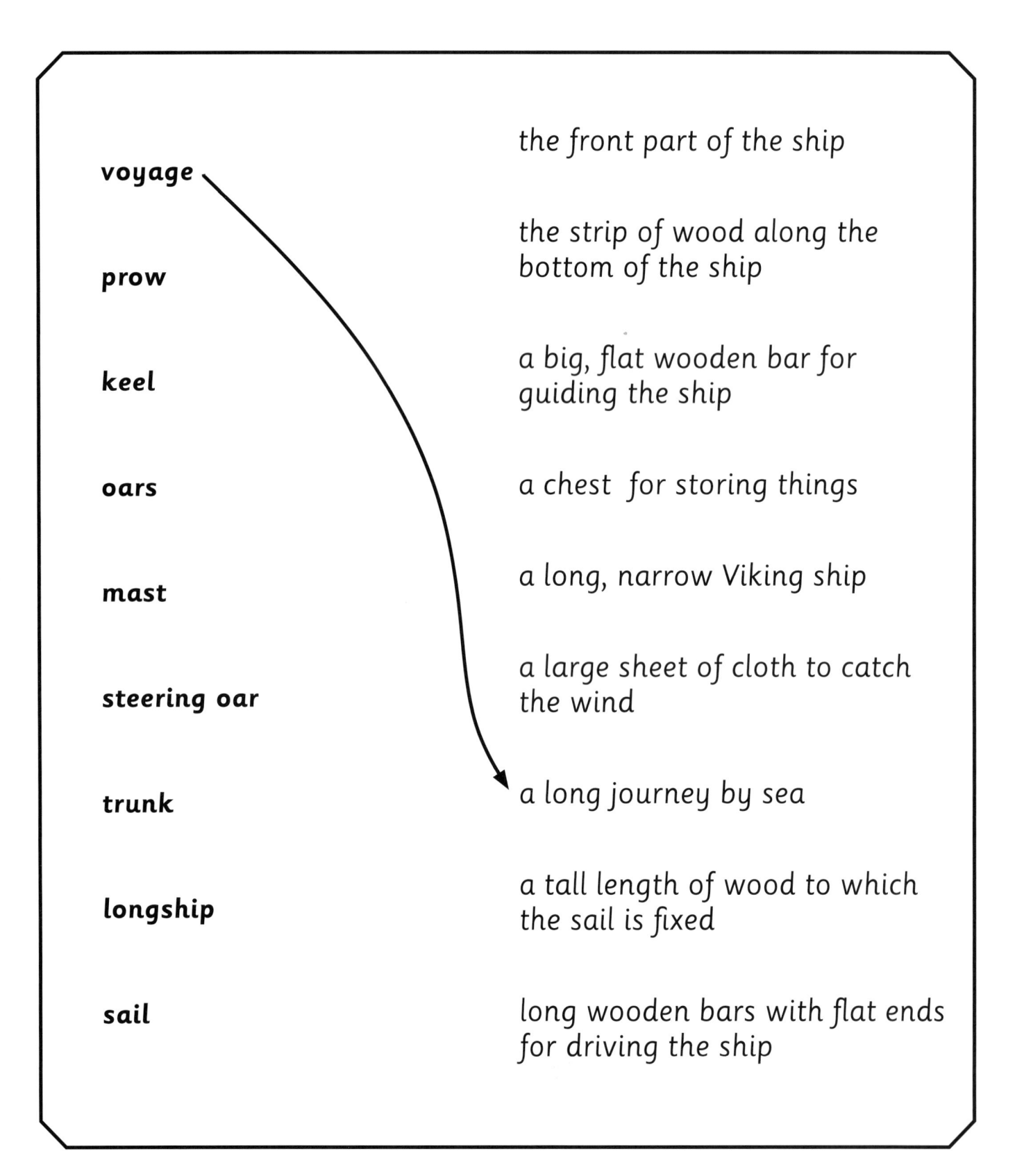

The Viking Longship 1

Memory work

What do these words mean? Can you remember?

Match them to their meanings by drawing a line like this.

voyage	the front part of the ship
prow	the strip of wood along the bottom of the ship
keel	a big, flat wooden bar for guiding the ship
oars	a chest for storing things
mast	a long, narrow Viking ship
steering oar	a large sheet of cloth to catch the wind
trunk	a long journey by sea
longship	a tall length of wood to which the sail is fixed
sail	long wooden bars with flat ends for driving the ship

voyage is matched to *a long journey by sea*.

The Viking Longship 2

Teacher's Notes
This and the following unit are designed to be used together.

Background

'Viking' originally comes from the Old Norse 'vikingr' – the word 'vik' means 'creek'. However, the name became synonymous with 'sea-raider'. Having travelled to distant places from Scandinavia, the longships also enabled the Vikings to negotiate coastal rocks and to travel through shallow water and along estuaries. As discussed in the unit 'Who were the Vikings?', the ship was originally designed to sail along fjords and into the open sea. Although most early raids in Britain were confined to the coastal regions, the ship could travel upriver if necessary. Sails could be lowered, oars set in place and under cover of darkness or mist surprise attacks could be made. Later the Vikings came in larger fleets. They established coastal bases, made raids inland on horseback and returned to their bases or chose to settle in the regions that they had invaded.

Working with the resource

'Upriver'
Here the same longship as drawn in 'On the open sea' is travelling along a river and is being driven by oars. You may wish to refer to the other illustration for comparison. Note also the shields set along the side of the ship.

Useful questions

1 Can you guess where the ship is? On the sea? In a river? Where?
2 How is it being driven?
3 What are the Vikings sitting on?
4 Can you find the sail? What has happened to it?
5 How are the two pictures, 'Upriver' and 'On the open sea' different?

Using the activity sheets

'Viking warrior'
The warrior can be labelled using the words given. The children could colour the clothes and also the shield, which would have been painted in bright colours. Some could add extra information, such as the materials used. Clothes were made from linen or wool. Shoes and belts were made from leather.

'Sea raiders'
The children can use what they have learned to complete the writing frame describing the arrival of the Viking raiders. Useful words are given. You could extend the work to discuss whether or not the Anglo-Saxon children reach their village in time.

The Viking Longship 2

Upriver

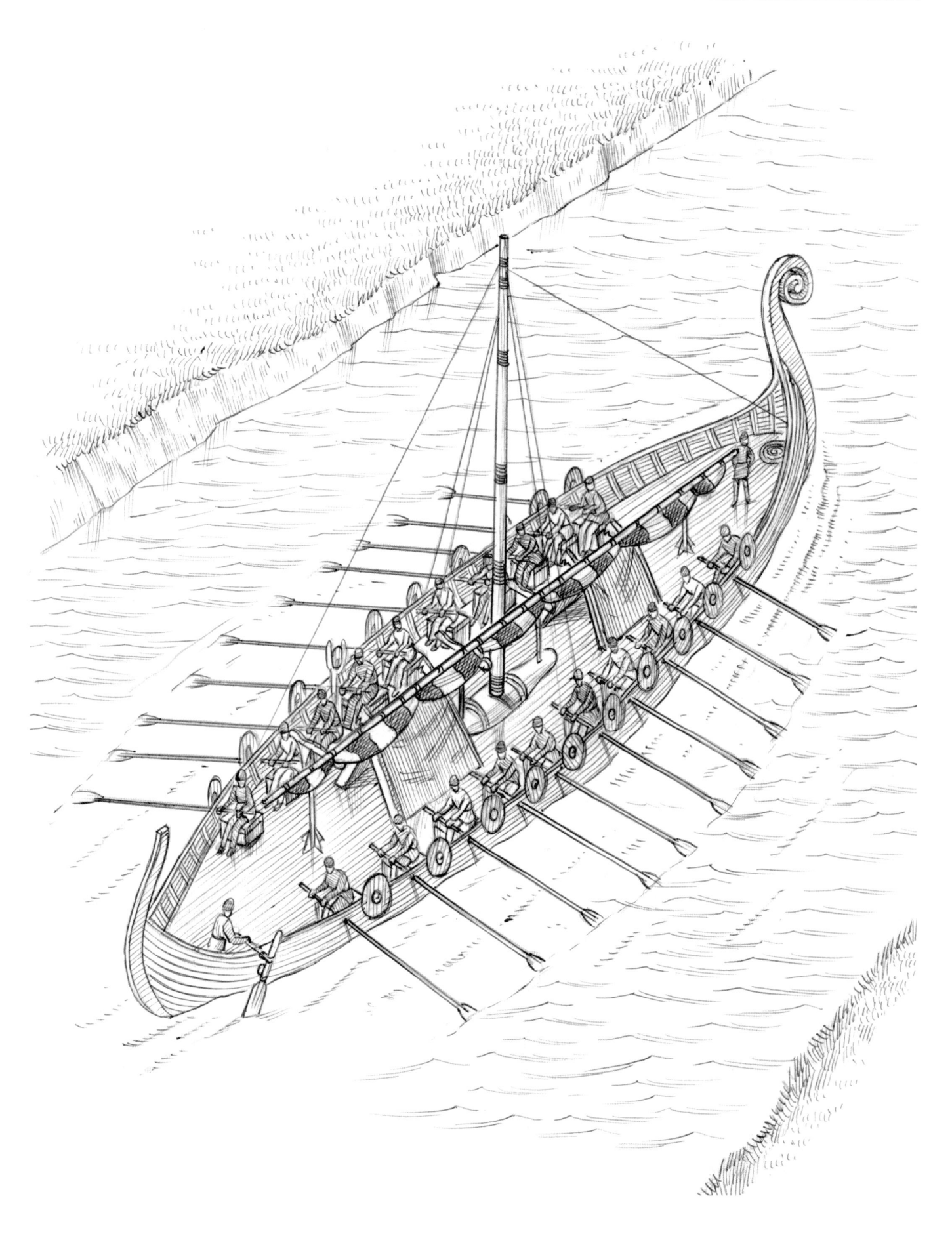

A longship being oar driven

The Viking Longship 2

Viking warrior

Label the Viking warrior with these words

    cloak   tunic   trousers   shoes   belt   brooch

    helmet   shield   spear   axe   sword   knife

A Viking warrior

© Folens (copiable page)   PRIMARY SPECIALS! *Invaders and Settlers in Britain*

The Viking Longship 2

Sea raiders

Imagine you are an Anglo-Saxon child. It is evening and you are by the riverbank with a friend.

Finish the writing frame.

Suddenly in the distance we saw …

The first longship was …

It came from …

The sail was down and …

We could see all their …

Quickly we turned and ran towards …

There was not much time …

Useful words

Vikings   sailing   creeping   bay   oars   swishing   water

shields   weapons   warn   village   families

---

60   PRIMARY SPECIALS! *Invaders and Settlers in Britain*   © Folens (copiable page)

Jorvik

Background

Despite their reputation as bloodthirsty warriors, the Vikings had an advanced culture and adapted easily to other cultures, intermarrying and adopting new ideas. Eoforvik, the Anglo-Saxon York, was re-named Jorvik after the Vikings settled there around 866, and it became a flourishing town. Excavations at the Coppergate site have revealed houses, workshops and numerous artefacts. This was largely due to the damp conditions, so that normally perishable goods, such as leather and textiles, have been preserved along with pots, bonework, woodwork and metalwork. These artefacts also reveal that there must have been established trade routes from Jorvik to many parts of the world. For example, silk from the Far East has been found at Coppergate. Buildings appear to have been organised in rows and included houses and workshops. Craftsmen and their families would have lived on the premises.

Working with the resource

'The bone-carver's workshop'

In the illustration the bone-carver is making a comb. His family are also included. Numerous products would have been made and a selection is shown in the workshop. Antlers and pieces of bone from cattle, horses and sheep can be seen along with horns. His tools, a saw for cutting bone, a small axe, a chisel and a file, are on the table. He is using a small hammer.

Useful questions

1 What is the craftsman making?
2 What is he making it from?
3 What jewellery has he made? (A bracelet, a brooch.)
4 What kind of musical instrument has he made? (A whistle.)
5 What else can you see? (Spoon, box, buckle, needles, dice, drinking horn.)
6 Do you know what the tools are he is using?

Using the activity sheets

'A Viking comb'

This is a simplified version of how the bone-carver would have made his comb but the essential details are included. The children can follow the diagram to help them and also search for the number cues at the start of the sentences.

'Names and nicknames'

The children can create names and nicknames for the Viking family from the information on the page. You may wish to encourage them to choose nicknames that would suit the individual members (such as 'bear-cub', 'wolf-cub' or 'piglet' for the children and 'jawbone' for the father whose trade is a bone-carver). They can go on to create other names or make up their own.

Jorvik

The bone-carver's workshop

A bone-carver's workshop

A Viking comb

Lots of Viking combs have been found. They were made by bone-carvers.

Number the sentences in the correct order to show how the bone-carver makes the comb.
Look at the pictures to help you.

Second, he cuts two long strips for the handle.

Fourth, he carves a pattern on the strips.

First, he cuts some rectangles from antlers.

Last of all, he cuts the rectangles to make teeth.

Fifth, he fixes the rectangles on to the strips with rivets.

Third, he makes the long strips smooth.

Jorvik

Names and nicknames

The Vikings loved nicknames. Here are some famous ones.

Eric Bloodaxe   **Thorkell the Tall**   **Swein Forkbeard**

- Choose first names for the Viking family in 'The bone-carver's workshop'.

- Then choose nicknames to match. Write them down below.

Male names	Female names	Nicknames
Grim	Bera	axe-blade
Hal	Dalla	battle-tooth
Ivor	Finna	bear-cub
Jarl	Gudrun	codfish-biter
Olaf	Helga	dove-nose
Rolf	Ingrid	dream-reader
Snorri	Kirstin	jawbone
		piglet
		red-cloak
		ring-slinger
		wag-beard
		wolf-cub